First
Facts™

Why in the World?

Why Do Geese Fly South in Winter?

A Book about Migration

by Kathy Allen

Consultant:
David Stokes
Associate Professor, Environmental Studies
Sonoma State University
Rohnert Park, California

Capstone press®

Mankato, Minnesota

First Facts is published by Capstone Press,
151 Good Counsel Drive, P.O. Box 669, Mankato, Minnesota 56002.
www.capstonepress.com

Library of Congress Cataloging-in-Publication Data
Allen, Kathy.
   Why do geese fly south in winter? : a book about migration / Kathy Allen.
   p. cm.—(First facts. Why in the world?)
   Summary: "A brief explanation of migration, including what it is, why and how animals
migrate, and how people affect migration"—Provided by publisher.
   Includes bibliographical references and index.
   ISBN-13: 978-0-7368-6380-3 (hardcover)
   ISBN-10: 0-7368-6380-X (hardcover)
   1. Animal migration—Juvenile literature. I. Title. II. Series.
QL754.A52 2007
591.56'8—dc22   2005037720

Editorial Credits

Jennifer Besel, editor; Juliette Peters, designer; Wanda Winch, photo researcher;
   Scott Thoms, photo editor

Photo Credits

Corbis/Buddy Mays, 13; George McCarthy, 11; Philip James Corwin, 18
Digital Vision, 8
Folio Inc./Everett Johnson, 21; Pat Lanza, 10
Getty Images Inc./The Image Bank/Joseph Van Os, 9
Houserstock/Dave G. Houser, 6–7
Minden Pictures/Foto Natura/Hans Schouten, cover; Frans Lanting, 20; Michael Quinton, 15, 16
Peter Arnold/Chlaus Lotscher, 4; Fred Bruemmer, 17; Tom Vezo, 12
Shutterstock/Ivan Histand, 5

1 2 3 4 5 6 11 10 09 08 07 06

Table of Contents

What Are These Animals Doing?

Marching over the bare ground, caribou move to the evergreen forests. Monarch butterflies flutter by on their long trip to Mexico. Canada geese soar high over your home, honking all the way.

What are all these animals doing? They're **migrating**.

Scientific Inquiry

Asking questions and making observations like the ones in this book are how scientists begin their research. They follow a process known as scientific inquiry.

Ask a Question

You see fewer squirrels in winter. You wonder, do squirrels migrate?

Investigate

Begin looking for squirrels in fall. Use a calendar to record how many squirrels you see each day. Use a hand lens to look for squirrel tracks on the ground, especially in the snow. Finally, read this book to learn why some animals migrate.

Explain

You see fewer squirrels in winter, but you still see some. You also know that squirrels have been around, because you see their tracks in the snow. You decide that squirrels do not migrate in winter. Record your findings in a notebook and remember to keep asking questions!

Why Do Geese Fly South in Winter?

Migrating animals travel between two **habitats**. Some animals move when the weather gets bad. They go to places where it's warmer. Many birds, like geese, move to the warm south in winter. In spring, they migrate back.

 Did you know?
Some insects migrate downward. Termites and earthworms migrate deep into the ground to escape the cold winter weather.

Some animals migrate to find food
and water. If these wildebeest didn't
move, they might starve or die of thirst.

Other animals migrate to **mate**. Penguins return to the shores where they were born. After they have their chicks, they head back to the water.

Why Doesn't My Dog Migrate?

So why don't all animals migrate?
Pets don't need to migrate. You give them
all the food, care, and shelter they need.

hibernating dormouse

Not all wild animals migrate, either. Some animals **hibernate** through long, cold winters. Other animals store food in their homes before winter comes.

scarlet tanager

How Do Animals Know When to Leave?

Some animals get very hungry before their migration. They eat and eat and eat! The animals get chubby as they store up fat for their long trips.

Season changes can also tell an animal to migrate. When days or nights get longer, the animals **sense** it's time to go.

monarch butterfly

13

Do Migrating Animals Have a Map?

Animals that migrate have an amazing ability to find their way. They use their senses and their **instincts**. Salmon use scents to find the way to their stream homes. Other animals follow the same routes every year. They remember certain trees or lakes along the way.

? Did you know?
Scientists think birds watch the stars to find their way at night. Sometimes, heavy fog or strong storms block out the stars, and the birds get lost.

chinook salmon

How Long Does Migration Take?

It can take animals a long time to get where they're going. Arctic terns spend six months migrating every year. They fly all the way from the Arctic to Antarctica in the fall. In the spring, they fly back.

Red crabs live on Christmas Island
in the Indian Ocean. Hundreds of crabs
migrate to the ocean, then back to land.
Their migration takes only a few days.

Do People Affect Migration?

Yes! In California, dams made by people block some rivers. Pacific salmon can't get past the dams to mate. Every year, fewer salmon swim in the rivers.

If animals can't follow their migration routes, they can't survive. People can help these animals by keeping migration paths clear.

> **? Did you know?**
> Pacific salmon are born in freshwater streams, then migrate to ocean waters. They return to the streams where they were born just before dying.

Soaring on their tiny wings, monarch butterflies migrate at least 2,500 miles (4,000 kilometers). As the butterflies migrate from Canada, they battle winds and fly around mountains. Finally, these amazing insects arrive in Mexico, where they land in the same trees every year.

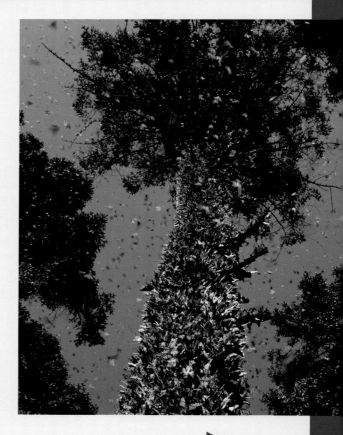

WHAT DO YOU THINK?

Every winter, snowbirds "migrate" from cold northern states to the warmer southern states. Then in the spring they go back to their homes in the north. But these snowbirds aren't birds. They're people. Maybe your grandparents are snowbirds. Do you think their migration is the same as animal migration?

GLOSSARY

habitat (HAB-uh-tat)—the place and natural conditions in which plants and animals live

hibernate (HYE-bur-nate)—to spend winter in a deep sleep

instinct (IN-stingkt)—behavior that an animal knows at birth and does not have to learn

mate (MATE)—to join together to produce young

migrate (MYE-grate)—to move from one place to another when seasons change or when food is scarce

sense (SENSS)—to feel or be aware of something; animals use the senses of sight, hearing, touch, taste, and smell to migrate.

READ MORE

Crossingham, John, and Bobbie Kalman. *What Is Migration?* The Science of Living Things. New York: Crabtree, 2002.

Hoff, Mary. *Migration.* World of Wonder. Mankato, Minn.: Creative Education, 2003.

Knight, Tim. *Marvelous Migrators.* Amazing Nature. Chicago: Heinemann, 2003.

INTERNET SITES

FactHound offers a safe, fun way to find Internet sites related to this book. All of the sites on FactHound have been researched by our staff.

Here's how:

1. Visit *www.facthound.com*

2. Choose your grade level.

3. Type in this book ID **073686380X** for age-appropriate sites. You may also browse subjects by clicking on letters, or by clicking on pictures and words.

4. Click on the **Fetch It** button.

FactHound will fetch the best sites for you!

INDEX